Y0-CAY-384

Dedication

BUILDING CYBER-READY WORKERS FROM A YOUNG AGE TO MEET NATIONAL WORKFORCE DEMANDS OF THE FUTURE
December 2016

This book is dedicated to supporting the workforce needs for the 21st century in the areas of cybersecurity. Some surveys estimate that there were over 200,000 cybersecurity jobs left unfilled in 2015 and the demand will grow exponentially over the next 20 years. This book, and subsequent episodes, will educate and inspire a new generation of potential cyber technologists, workers and managers who will have had the opportunity to experience the cybersecurity territory from early childhood thus making "cyber speak" and careers in this area much less foreign.

The book targets children between the ages of 8 and 12, as well as adults who like to read with them. Everyone can benefit from reading these episodes in order to become safer online.

McGarry (2013) reported that General Keith Alexander, former Director, NSA, described cybersecurity work as a "tremendous opportunity" for young people…" He said - "This generation is coming up cyber savvy," after explaining how his almost 2-year-old granddaughter knows how to use an iPad to watch movies on Netflix. "We can train them. We can educate them."

Source: McGarry, B. (Oct. 14, 2013). NSA Chief: What Cyberwarrior Shortage?

ACKNOWLEDGMENTS

To all of my friends, family, colleagues and supporters of this effort, I thank you dearly.

~ and ~

To Roy, who fully supported all of my ideas with kindness, respect and endless love.

Jastin is twelve years old and is a very active child on the Internet. In the last Phishing and Ransomware episode, he got in big trouble clicking on the wrong email causing his family to have to pay $2,000 in ransom to an unknown hacker who took control of the family computer. Under the guidance of Super Cybersecurity Grandma (*Super Cee Gee*), the experience taught the entire family a few things like: being careful about suspicious emails and being vigilant by keeping a backup of important information on their computers.

This lesson also helped Jastin's dad at his job where they hold something called Cybersecurity Awareness Training for all employees to make sure that the company's information, employee privacy and trade secrets stay secure. To test to see if the employees are actually learning something, the computer department at Dad's job often sends out "phishing" emails disguised as coming from outside the company to all of the employees to see if they will click on the suspicious link. This way, they can tell if the employees are actually listening to the cybersecurity awareness training or just sleeping on the job!

Well, Jastin's Dad passed the test at work with flying colors because he had learned - the hard way - about being hacked at home with the ransomware incident. His boss praised him for not falling for the phishing email because as many as 1 out of 5 people who should know better, still click and get themselves (and the company) in trouble!

Dad was so excited that he bragged and bragged about his super-smart son who taught the family about some dangers of being online. He told everyone who would listen, even the parents of

Jastin's schoolmates. The parents passed on the bragging to Jastin's schoolmates until just about everyone was tired of hearing about it!

Also, Jastin's dad was so excited about having the right answers at work, he was not angry with him anymore and allowed him to use the family computer again, long before his punishment was over.

So, forgetting that the original phishing email came from the "Let's go hunting for Special Animals in Your Neighborhood" – **www.neighborhoodanimals.org** website, Jastin continued his animal hunt project. He took more pictures of things in the neighborhood, like a rabbit on top of his mailbox and his mom standing in the front door holding their pet cat. While walking to school, he took pictures along the way of all the cool animals he saw in the neighborhood and in front of the school.

1214 Main Street
Anytown, USA

Thinking that they were "out of the woods" with this cybersecurity stuff, life was good again for Jastin and his family.

Until one day – Jastin went to his social media site and saw the following posted by someone he didn't know:

"JASTIN IS STUPID – HE THINKS HE IS SO SMART – HIS DAD TALKS ABOUT HIM TOO MUCH – LET'S GET HIM WHEN HE GETS TO SCHOOL TOMORROW!

WE WILL TEACH HIM A LESSON ABOUT SHOWING US UP!"

The next day, Jastin was "scarrreeed" to death about going to school. He wore clothes to cover up his head; he wore dark glasses thinking the mean person wouldn't be able to recognize him.

He made it through the day. Whew! But after dinner, he looked at his phone and there was a text message where Jastin saw:

JASTIN – YOU DIDN'T GET AWAY TODAY;

WE WILL GET YOU TOMORROW FOR BEING SO

SMART AND MAKING EVERYONE LOOK BAD!!!!!

At this point, Jastin had to do something. He couldn't continue hiding forever.

He started to think and, all of a sudden, he remembered what he heard about being picked on by unknown people at a presentation in the school auditorium. Yes, it all connected! What was happening to him was called **CYBER BULLYING**.

At school he heard about cyber bullies threatening and saying inappropriate things online about girls and boys - making it emotionally difficult and tragic for some children in other states

- so bad that it pushed victims to the point of hurting themselves. Jastin didn't want those things happening to him. He also remembered that the speaker at school said that if someone was bothering you online, the first thing you should do is to tell your family or teachers. So that's what he did!

Jastin went straight to *Super Cee Gee* who told him not to hide when he went to school the next day. She told him to be smart and look out for things that might give him clues about who the cyber bully might be.

She told him to repeat to other students what he heard at the assembly about cyber bullying and to anyone who would listen. He was to talk about how bad it was for everyone, and that we shouldn't say bad things about people when talking to them in person or online.

She said that if anyone tried to bother him to let them know that parents and schools are aware of cyber bullies because it has been in the news a lot.

She urged Jastin to stand up to them and let him or her know that they would get in trouble AND get their parents in trouble with the law too!

He should also tell everyone that the police can find out information from the phone and email address that cyber bullies use – so they can be Found Out!

Well, as time went on, Jastin actually became a spokesperson for cyber bullying in his class. Over and over, he let everyone know the right things to do to NOT become a cyber bully in the first place, *AND* the right things to do if a cyber bully bothers you.

Once again, *Super Cee Gee*, Jastin and his family learned just a little more about being safe online by following some very simple rules:

1. Always be kind to others online and in-person.
2. Limit the amount of information you share about yourself and your family in the online arena.
3. Cyber bullying has become very popular, so be sure to learn as much as you can about it to keep you, and your friends and family safe.
4. Encourage your school, club or church to invite an expert to talk to the students about what to do about cyber bullying.
5. Let someone you trust know if you become a victim of cyber bullying.

Jastin and his family, of course, are not 100% safe from Internet risks, threats, and vulnerabilities, as they still do things online that are not totally careful. But will any of us ever be 100% secure?

Stay tuned to the next episode where *Super Cee Gee*, Jastin and his family continue to work out the cybersecurity issues related to the 'Internet of Things" (IoT) . IoT is a new and exciting arena that we have entered into with all of the internet-connected devices we may own and now have in our homes. Also, Jastin is still not being careful about posting personal family information – more to come on that!!!

Glossary

Backup – Backing up your computers and mobile devices to offline storage is an important step that everyone should take on a regular basis. It is important in case you lose access to the information on your device. There are many ways to save data, like on external hard drives, USB drives, and even what is called backing up to "The Cloud". Any of these methods will allow you to get your information if your computer "crashes" or is taken for "ransom."

Computer Security Awareness Training – It is very important for companies, schools, and other organizations to train employees and students to be careful about being on the Internet at work and when using e-mail. People within the organization can make mistakes that can cause the company to lose information about their products, services and employee personal information. So, they conduct Computer Security Awareness Training to help people be aware of the dangers.

Cyber Bullying – This term is often used to describe many undesirable activities related to the internet, social media, e-mail and texting. The term is derived from traditional bullying in school, where children were threatened and mistreated in various ways. With so much use of the internet now, the bullying activities take on a different form but the negative influences and actions are similar and more pervasive. As such, it has become very difficult to monitor and curtail. Everyone must be aware of this phenomenon so that cyber bully victims can be protected and cyber bullies can be taught to respect others.

Cybersecurity – Today, we perform many tasks on our computers and mobile devices and are totally in the "digital age." Because of this, it is important for us to do as much as we can to protect the confidentiality and privacy of our information, to prevent our information from being taken or changed and, to keep our devices and equipment up and running. Cybersecurity is just this – formally called confidentiality, integrity, and availability. The country needs skilled people to work in the many technical and non-technical fields that support these efforts.

Internet of Things (IoT) - For a while, computers communicated through "addresses," that used something called IPv4 across networks (you will learn about this later). With the implementation of IPv6 (something you will also learn about later), the world now has many device "addresses" that can be associated with not only computers and networks, but with many, many other items like cars, refrigerators, alarm systems and mobile devices. Since "things" can now communicate over the internet – this term - IoT was coined. This is a good thing, but with so many devices talking to each other and possibly sharing personal information, we need to think about some of the cybersecurity dangers since we easily buy and install them because of the conveniences they provide.

Internet Risks, Threats and Vulnerabilities – Everyone should know about the risks they are taking when they are online and try to understand what do to about the possibility of something bad happening. Threats are the bad things that can happen like viruses and malware, and phishing e-mails. A vulnerability is a "weak link" that allow threats to happen. An example of a vulnerability is having a computer or mobile phone without a password on it.

Social Media – This term describes the tools that we use to communicate with friends, family, and just about anyone online. Apps like Facebook, Snapchat, Instagram, Twitter, LinkedIn and many other sites have been great for students to communicate with their friends and for adults to communicate with people they work with. But many times, people use these apps in the wrong way, forgetting that everything that they put online can be read by anyone. Information that someone puts on their social media page can also haunt them later during college admissions and job searches. Interviewers look at social media sites and can use the information they find against you.

Super Cybersecurity Grandma Cyber Bullying Word Search

Find each of the following words

ABUSE	CYBERBULLYING	FEAR	ONLINE	HARASSMENT
HUMILIATE	DISCREDIT	PROBLEM	VICTIM	MANIPULATE
EMAIL	MESSAGE	DANGER	TEEN	CELLPHONE
TEENAGE	SOCIAL			

```
C  O  N  L  I  N  E  F  E  A  R  M  T  A  E
E  T  E  E  N  T  E  E  N  A  G  E  E  B  E
L  M  H  U  M  I  L  I  A  T  E  S  E  H  N
L  E  S  U  M  M  E  M  A  I  L  S  N  A  N
P  S  O  O  A  D  A  N  G  E  R  A  D  R  B
H  S  N  S  C  D  A  N  G  E  R  G  A  A  M
O  A  E  M  A  I  L  E  I  T  E  E  N  S  E
N  G  E  E  P  B  A  E  V  P  N  T  G  S  N
E  E  M  A  I  L  U  L  P  I  U  E  E  M  A
P  D  A  N  G  E  R  S  L  R  C  L  R  E  F
R  V  I  C  T  I  M  N  E  D  O  T  A  N  N
O  N  L  I  N  E  O  F  E  A  R  B  I  T  T
B  D  I  S  C  R  E  D  I  T  M  N  L  M  E
C  Y  B  E  R  B  U  L  L  Y  I  N  G  E  A
T  O  E  A  N  E  N  I  H  D  M  A  E  L  M
```

Made in the USA
Columbia, SC
25 July 2022

63957035R00018